VERSUS

FORD vs FERRARI
THE HIGH-SPEED FALLOUT

KENNY ABDO

Fly!
An Imprint of Abdo Zoom
abdobooks.com

abdobooks.com

Published by Abdo Zoom, a division of ABDO, P.O. Box 398166, Minneapolis, Minnesota 55343. Copyright © 2023 by Abdo Consulting Group, Inc. International copyrights reserved in all countries. No part of this book may be reproduced in any form without written permission from the publisher. Fly!™ is a trademark and logo of Abdo Zoom.

Printed in the United States of America, North Mankato, Minnesota.
102022
012023

Photo Credits: Alamy, AP Images, Getty Images, Shutterstock
Production Contributors: Kenny Abdo, Jennie Forsberg, Grace Hansen
Design Contributors: Candice Keimig, Neil Klinepier, Laura Graphenteen

Library of Congress Control Number: 2021950282

Publisher's Cataloging-in-Publication Data

Names: Abdo, Kenny, author.
Title: Ford vs. Ferrari: the high-speed fallout / by Kenny Abdo.
Other title: the high-speed fallout
Description: Minneapolis, Minnesota : Abdo Zoom, 2023 | Series: Versus | Includes online resources and index.
Identifiers: ISBN 9781098228637 (lib. bdg.) | ISBN 9781098229474 (ebook) | ISBN 9781098229894 (Read-to-Me ebook)
Subjects: LCSH: Ford Motor Company--Juvenile literature. | Ferrari automobile-History--Juvenile literature. | Automobiles, Racing--Juvenile literature. | Competition--Economic aspects--Juvenile literature.
Classification: DDC 338.7--dc23

TABLE OF CONTENTS

Ford vs. Ferrari 4

The Companies 8

Fight! 14

Legacy 18

Glossary 22

Online Resources 23

Index 24

FORD vs FERRARI

No other feud in history has been as fast paced as the one between car giants Ford and Ferrari!

What started as a simple business proposal ended in a race to the finish line for the fastest car.

THE COMPANIES

Ford Motor Company was founded by Henry Ford in 1903. Ford was the first to build cars for the public. Ford's grandson, Henry Ford II, became **CEO** of the company in 1945.

Enzo Ferrari began his career as a race car test driver. In 1946, he began designing his own race cars. After winning many **Grand Prix** races, Ferrari became known as the best on the track.

By 1963, Ferrari had fallen on hard times. Ford saw an opportunity to become not only the best car company in the US, but in the whole world!

FIGHT!

Ford offered to **buy out** Ferrari. The deal was rejected when Ferrari realized that he would lose control of his racing team.

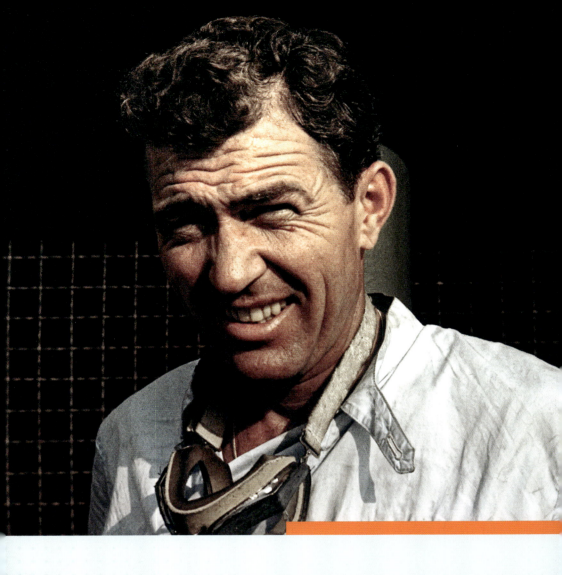

Feeling slighted, Ford contacted Carroll Shelby. He was a famous American race car builder at the time. Ford asked Shelby to develop a car that could beat Ferrari at the famous **Le Mans** race.

Ford also worked with British race car company Lola on the design. Together, they **unveiled** the Ford GT40 in 1964.

Ford easily defeated Ferrari at **Le Mans** in 1966. The Ford GT40 captured first, second, and third place! One of the cars was driven by British driver Ken Miles. Ferrari was left in the dust.

Ford v Ferrari, a film based on the feud, was released in 2019. It starred Matt Damon as Shelby and Christian Bale as Miles. It was nominated for Best Picture at the 92nd **Academy Awards**!

Ford remains a leader in **innovating** and improving personal transportation. Ferrari's cars continue to be in the top tier for racing.

Even decades after the **rift**, Ford defeating Ferrari is considered one of the greatest against-the-odds wins of all time!

GLOSSARY

Academy Awards – a yearly award ceremony that honors the best in American and international films.

buy out – to pay someone to give up ownership of something.

CEO – short for chief executive officer, the top person who is in charge of a company.

Grand Prix – a motorsport competition that began in France around 1890. It started as road races from one town to another. It turned into an endurance test for race cars and their drivers. More than 15 are held yearly around the world.

innovate – to come up with a new idea, method, or device.

Le Mans – also known as 24 Hours of Le Mans, a car race held annually near the town of Le Mans, France. It is the world's oldest endurance racing event.

rift – a break in friendly relations or a partnership.

unveil – to show publicly for the first time.

ONLINE RESOURCES

To learn more about Ford and Ferrari, please visit **abdobooklinks.com** or scan this QR code. These links are routinely monitored and updated to provide the most current information available.

INDEX

Bale, Christian 19

Damon, Matt 19

Ferrari, Enzo 11, 12, 14

Ford GT40 16, 27

Ford, Henry 9

Ford II, Henry 9, 12, 14, 15

Ford v Ferrari (movie) 19

Lola (company) 16

Miles, Ken 17, 19

Shelby, Carroll 15, 19

24 Hours of Le Mans 15, 17